# For *the* Glory *of* Christ

## SONGS FOR THE SOUL-WINNING CHURCH

*Arranged by*
### MIKE SPECK,
#### DANNY ZALOUDIK, *and* CLIFF DUREN

*Orchestrated by*
#### J. DANIEL SMITH, DANNY ZALOUDIK,
#### and CHRIS McDONALD

**LILLENAS**
**PUBLISHING COMPANY**

lillenas.com

# CONTENTS

# We Have Come into This House

*with*
Praise the Lord
Come on and Praise Him

Words and Music by
MARK CONDEN
*Arranged by Mike Speck,*
*Cliff Duren and Danny Zaloudik*

**PLEASE NOTE: Copying of this product is NOT covered by CCLI licenses. For CCLI information call 1-800-234-2446.**

6

10

# Serve the Lord

*with*

## Joyful, Joyful, We Adore Thee

Words and Music by
GREG DAY and PHILIP ROBINSON
*Arranged by Mike Speck,*
*Cliff Duren and Danny Zaloudik*

**CD: 11**

fore Him___ now,_____ with thank - ful___ hearts, as we

lift up___ ho - ly hands._____ For He___ is

wor - thy to re - ceive glo - ry, hon - or___ and

pow - er, bless - ing and praise! For the Lord is good, His

truth for - ev - er reigns! Serve the Lord,

serve the Lord with glad - ness. Serve the Lord,

# All for the Glory of Christ

*with*
## I Am Not Ashamed

Words and Music by
**JOEL GUINNESS, TWILA McBRIDE-LaBAR
and KEVIN STOKES**
*Arranged by Mike Speck,
Cliff Duren and Danny Zaloudik*

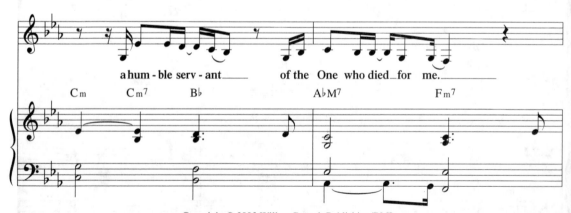

28

I will reach for the stars,_____ I will dream from the heart,_

I will reach for the stars,_____ I will dream from the heart,_

_____ do it all for the glo - ry__ of Christ._____

_____ do it all for the glo - ry of Christ._____

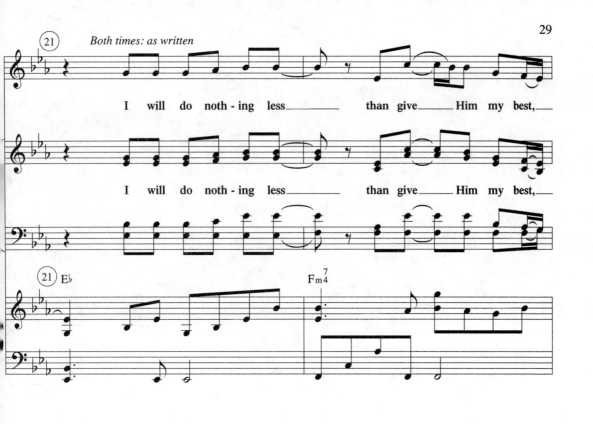

I will do noth-ing less_____ than give____ Him my best,____

I will do noth-ing less_____ than give____ Him my best,____

and live each day of my life_____ all for the glo - ry,

and live each day of my life_____ all for the glo - ry,

**CD: 19**

all for the glo - ry _____ of Christ. _____

*Divisi*

all for the glo - ry of Christ. _____

*Divisi*

C♭M9   B♭m7   E♭2   C♭M9   B♭m7

decresc.

*Solo*
*mp*

How could I live _____ for _____ my own self - ish gain _____

E♭2   B♭/A♭   A♭

*mp*

when I've dis - cov - ered _____ the rea - son I _____ was made? _____

Cm7   B♭2   B♭   A♭M9   Fm4/7

8vb - - - - - - - - - - - - - - - - - - - - - - - - - - - - - -

**CD: 20**

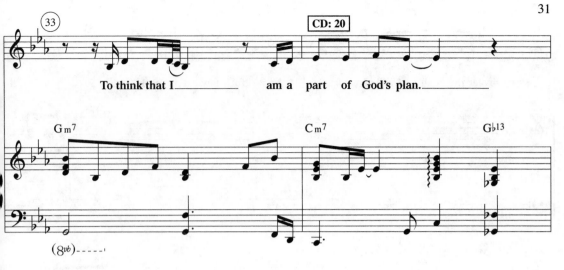

To think that I_____ am a part of God's plan._____

My heart's de - sire_____ is to o - bey His com - mand._____ What-

Oo_____

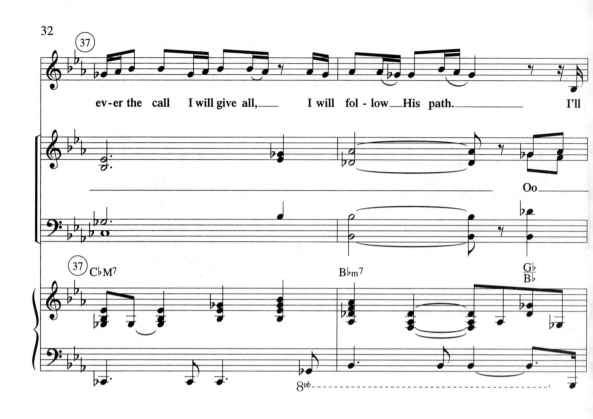

ev-er the call   I will give all,____   I will  fol - low____His path._____   I'll

Oo____

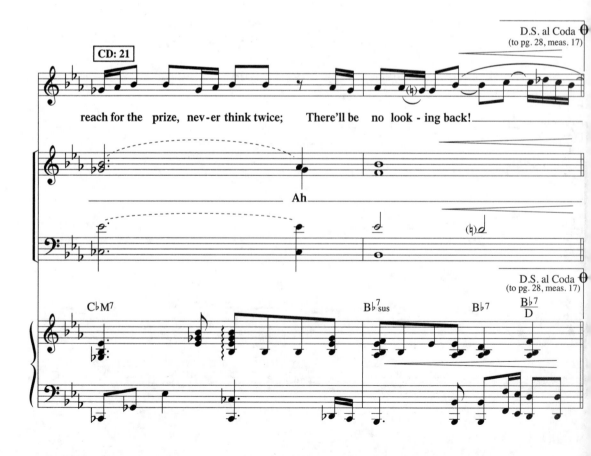

**CD: 21**

reach for the   prize,  nev - er think twice;   There'll be   no  look - ing back!____

Ah____

D.S. al Coda
(to pg. 28, meas. 17)

all for the glo - ry of Christ! I will

all for the glo - ry. What - ev - er the call, I will give all,

reach for the prize. It's not a - bout me, nev - er should be.

not a - bout me, nev - er should be.

34

*"I Am Not Ashamed"

I've got too much be-hind me to let this world blind me. To

I've got too much be-hind me to let this world blind me. To

CD: 23

some He's a name, but to me He's my ev-'ry-thing!

some He's a name, but to me He's my ev-'ry-thing!

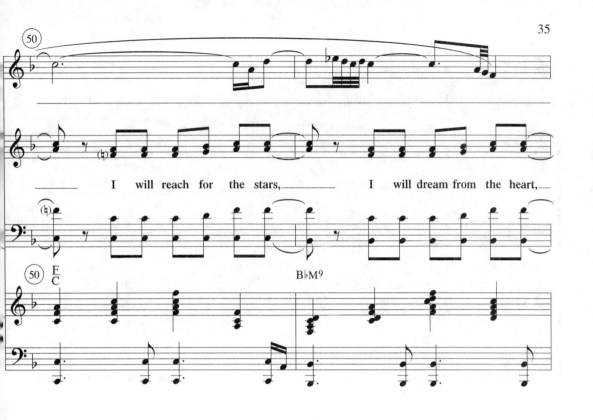

I will reach for the stars,_____ I will dream from the heart,

Do it all for the glo - ry of Christ._____

do it all for the glo - ry of Christ._____

36

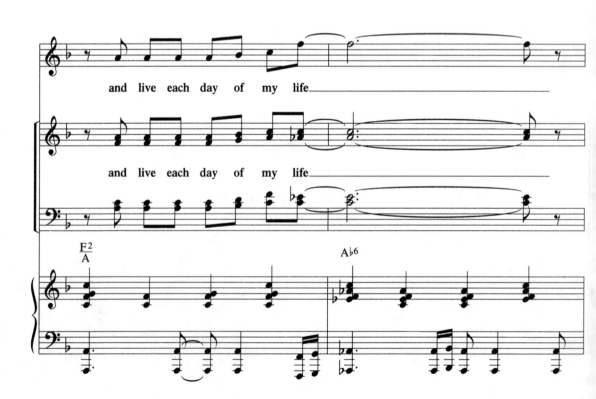

all for the glo - ry, all for the glo - ry,____

*Unison*

all for the glo - ry, all for the glo - ry,

*Unison*

Gm⁷      $\frac{F}{A}$     $\frac{F^2}{A}$

rit.

all for the glo - ry of Christ!____

*Divisi*

all for the glo - ry of Christ!____

*Divisi*

D♭M⁷    Cm⁷       F

rit.

# All the Glory Belongs to Jesus

GLORIA GAITHER

WILLIAM J. GAITHER
*Arranged by Mike Speck,*
*Cliff Duren and Danny Zaloudik*

# I'm a Soldier

*with*
I'm on the Battlefield
Keep on the Firing Line
Onward, Christian Soldiers

Words and Music
Unknown
*Arranged by Mike Speck,*
*Cliff Duren and Danny Zaloudik*

sol - dier___ in the ar-my of the Lord, I'm a sol - dier in the ar - my. I'm a sol - dier___ in the ar-my of the Lord, I'm a sol - dier in the ar - my. I'm a sol - dier___ in the

with separation

44

45

on the bat - tle - field for my Lord. I'm a

sol - dier_____ in the ar - my of the Lord, I'm a

sol - dier in the ar - my. I'm a

48

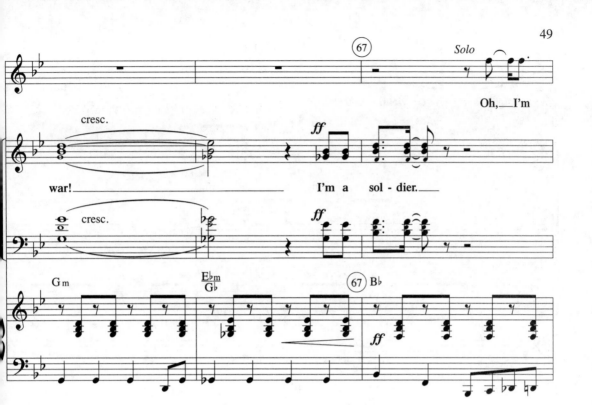

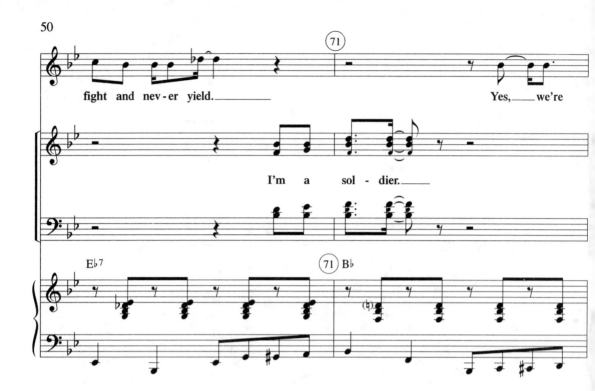

fight and nev-er yield._____ Yes,\_\_\_\_we're

I'm a sol - dier.\_\_\_\_\_

march-ing as to war. I'm a sol - dier in the\_\_\_\_ ar - my of\_\_\_ the\_\_\_

I'm a sol - dier in the ar - my of the

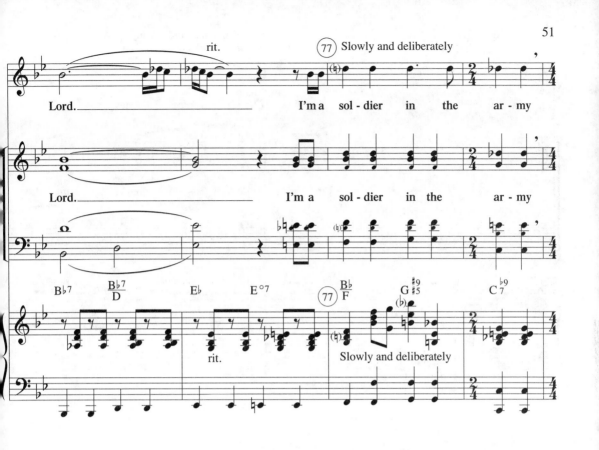

52

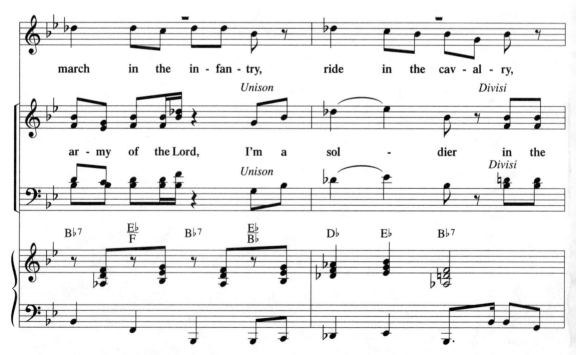

54

# Closet Religion

Words and Music by
**DOTTIE PEOPLES**
*Arranged by Mike Speck,*
*Cliff Duren and Danny Zaloudik*

I don't have a clos - et re - li - gion. I can't hide the

with separation

Da-ri-us signed a de-cree:_____ There___ won't

be no pray-in' 'round here._____

Who-so-ev-er calls___ on___ an-y god's name will be

cast in-to the li-ons den._____

Dan - iel did-n't pay the king___ no at - ten - tion. Three times a

day He prayed to God, an - y - way.___ When con-

front - ed with the con - se - quenc - es of the li - ons den___ I can

**CD: 37**

hear ol' Dan - iel say___ that I don't,

44 %  *Solo continues*
*Choir* f

(mel.)

I don't have a clos - et re - li - gion.   I can't hide the

44 Db7      Db7/F      Gb      Ab9sus      Db7      Db7/F   Db7/Ab

48

God I   serve.  I've got to   let the world know,____ wher - ev - er I go.____

Gb      Ab9sus      48 Db/Ab      Ab/Gb      Db/F      Bb7#9

CD: 38  1st time        CD: 40  2nd time        2nd time to Coda
                                                (to pg. 63, meas. 70)

I've   got to   praise__ and   serve____ the Lord, Oo,   serve   the

N.C.  Db9/F   Bb7#5   Eb7b9      Ab9      N.C.        2nd time to Coda
                                                     (to pg. 63, meas. 70)

Lord.

All night Dan - iel stayed in the li - on's

den. And in the morn - in', to the king's sur - prise,

God sent His an - gels to

Oo

I'm gon - na let it shine._____ Oh,_____

I'm gon - na let it shine._____

hide it un-der a bush-el, no. I'm gon-na let it shine._

Hide it un-der a bush-el, no. I'm gon-na let it shine._

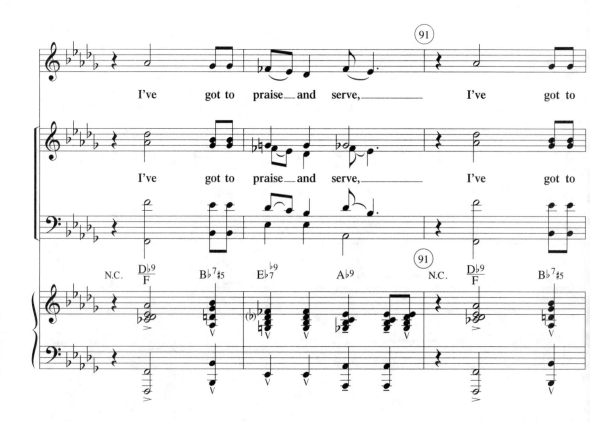

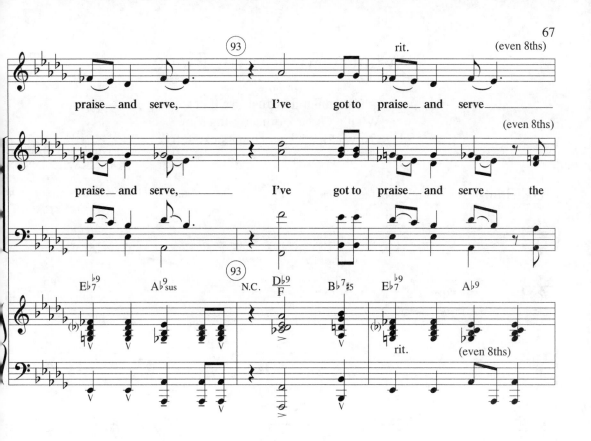

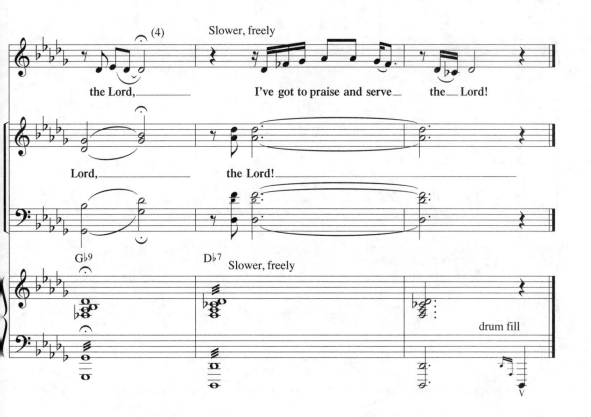

# What a Wonderful Place

*with*

Canaanland Is Just in Sight
What a Great Homecoming Day
I've Never Been This Homesick Before

Words and Music by
DIANNE WILKINSON
*Arranged by Mike Speck*
*Cliff Duren and Danny Zaloudik*

**CD: 41** Bright Southern Gospel feel ♩ = ca. 136

When I first start-ed out____to serve Je-sus, there in His Word I read of a place; Cit-y of

**PLEASE NOTE: Copying of this product is NOT covered by CCLI licenses. For CCLI information call 1-800-234-2446.**

day when I hear the Lord___ call._____ What a won-der-ful

place     is    wait - ing   when I   cross___ to    the oth - er side.

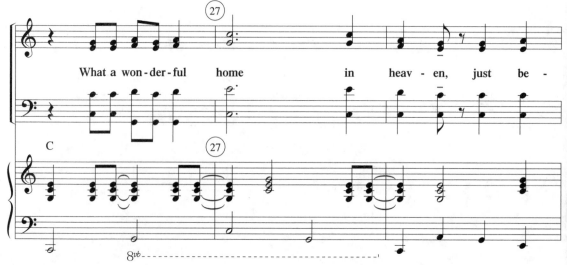

What a won-der-ful     home      in   heav - en,   just   be -

yond that great di - vide. What a won-der-ful hope e -

ter - nal through His mer - cy and His grace. What a won-der-ful

cit-y, won-der-ful home, what a won-der-ful place!

CD: 43

72

**"Canaanland Is Just in Sight"**

Unison  
There will be no sorrow, there in that tomorrow.

We will be there, by and by,

by and by. What a

*"What a Great Homecoming Day"

great home-com-ing day, what a day in heav-en 'twill be when we

bid this world good-bye, and our home, at last we

see, we will see! See___ the bright___

74

62 *"I've Never Been This Homesick Before"

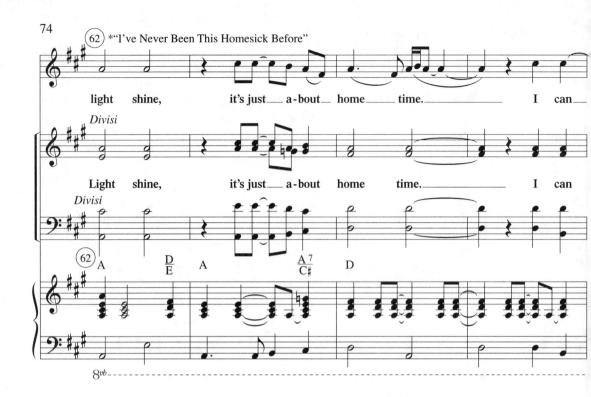

light shine, it's just a-bout home time. I can

Divisi

Light shine, it's just a-bout home time. I can

Divisi

62 A  D/E  A  A7/C#  D

8vb

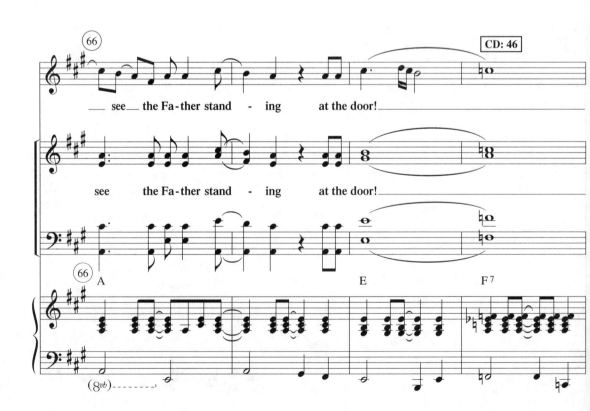

66  CD: 46

see the Fa-ther stand - ing at the door!

see the Fa-ther stand - ing at the door!

66 A  E  F7

(8vb)

What a won-der-ful, what a won-der-ful What a won-der-ful

*Unison* *Divisi*

What a won-der-ful, what a won-der-ful place is

*Unison* *Divisi*

F⁷ N.C.  F♯⁷ N.C.  B  E F♯

place!

wait - ing when I cross___ to the oth - er side. What a won-der-ful

B  E  B

What a won-der-ful home.

home in heav - en, just be - yond that great di-

**CD: 47**

What a won-der-ful, what a won-der-ful

vide.

What a won-der-ful, what a won-der-ful

hope e - ter - nal through His mer - cy and His

*Divisi*

hope e - ter - nal through His mer - cy and His

*Divisi*

grace. What a won - der - ful cit - y, a won - der - ful

grace. What a won - der - ful cit - y, won - der - ful

home,—what a won-der-ful place! What a won-der-ful
Home-com-ing day!
home, what a won-der-ful place! What a won-der-ful
Home-com-ing day!

Eb9 Ab7 Db Dbsus/Eb Db/F Gb G°7

cit-y, a won-der-ful home, what a won-der-ful
cit-y, won-der-ful home,

Db/Ab Bb7 Eb9 Ab13 N.C.

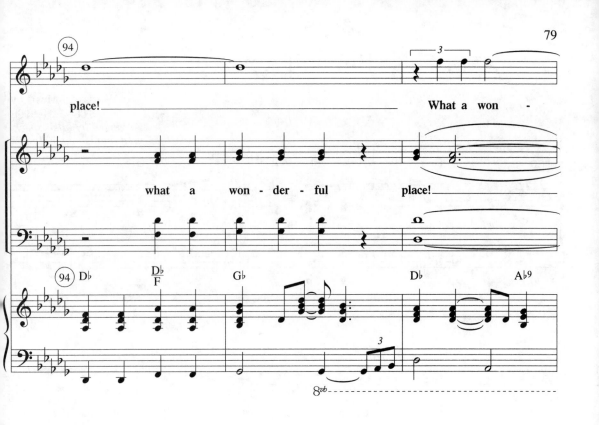

# I'm Still Amazed

Words and Music by
**STEVE HURTE**
*Arranged by Mike Speck,*
*Cliff Duren and Danny Zaloudik*

**PLEASE NOTE: Copying of this product is NOT covered by CCLI licenses. For CCLI information call 1-800-234-2446.**

still at a loss why He'd take the cross in -

stead____ of a street of pure____ gold._____ He's the

on - ly__ King who gave____ ev - 'ry - thing in ex -

Choir

Oo_____

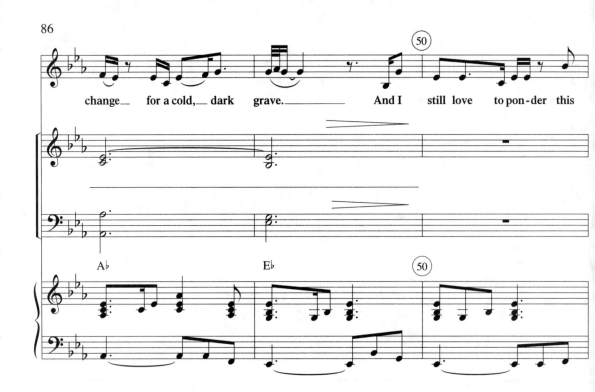

change__ for a cold,__ dark grave._____ And I still love to pon-der this

**CD: 52**

God giv-en won-der, O__ yes, I'm still a - mazed._____ I'm a -

O yes, I'm still a - mazed._____ I'm a -

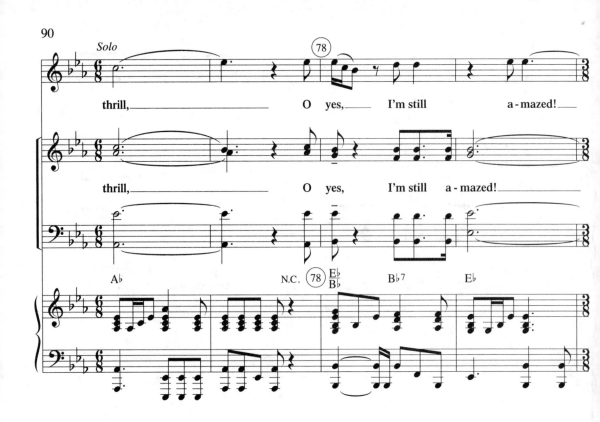

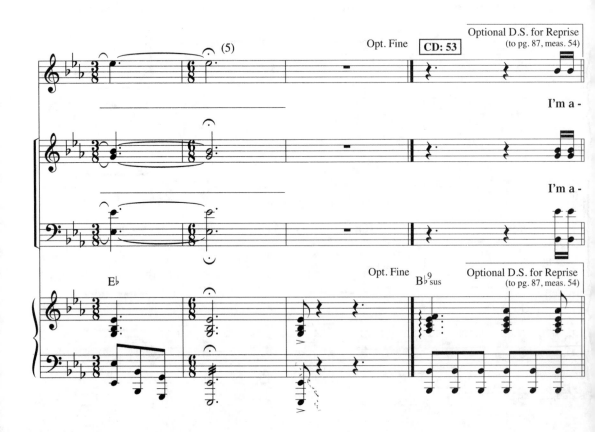

# Jesus Saves

Words and Music by
**DARYL WILLIAMS**
**and STEPHEN HILL**
*Arranged by Mike Speck,*
*Cliff Duren and Danny Zaloudik*

Ev - 'ry drop of blood that touched the ground cried Je - sus saves, Je - sus saves. A

world of sin___ re-joiced___ to hear the sound___ that Je - sus

F♯   B/F♯   B2/F♯   F♯   D♯m7

**CD: 55**

saves,   Je - sus saves.

G♯m7   C♯2/E♯   C♯/E♯   F♯

*with more emotion*

E - ven the sword___ that pierced His side   cried___ Je - sus

G   C/G   G   Em

saves,   Je - sus saves.   The

D   D/F♯   G   C/G

I've been par-doned, full and free.

I've been par-doned, full and free.

D    D7/F#    G    D9sus

All be-cause the blood still sings, Je-

All be-cause the blood still sings, Je-sus

G    Am7    G/B    Em    Am7

In the Book of Life, beside my name is Je-

Oo

Ah

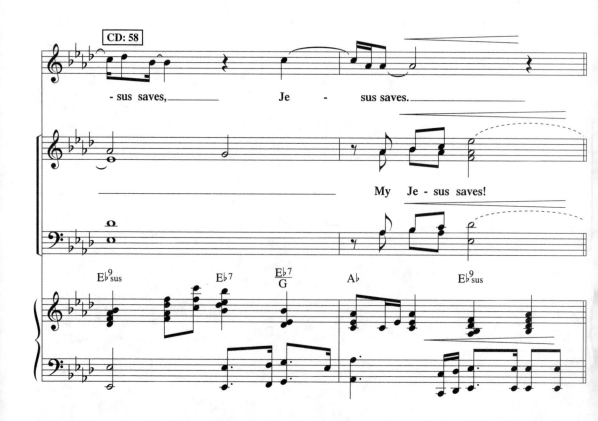

- sus saves, Je - sus saves.

My Je - sus saves!

Hal - le - lu - jah, I'm re - deemed.

Hal - le - lu - jah, I'm re - deemed.

Ab    Bbm7    Ab/C    Fm7

I've been par - doned, full and free.

I've been par - doned, full and free.

Bbm7    Eb/G    Ab    Eb9sus

All be - cause___ the blood___ still sings,_____ Je - sus

All be - cause the blood still sings,_____ Je - sus

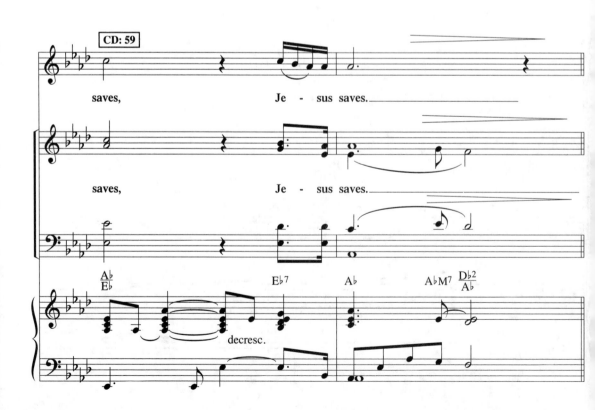

saves, Je - sus saves._____

saves, Je - sus saves._____

# I Wish I Could Have Been There

Word
WAYNE HAUN and JOEL LINDSAY
*Arranged by Mike Speck,*
*Cliff Duren and Danny Zaloudik*

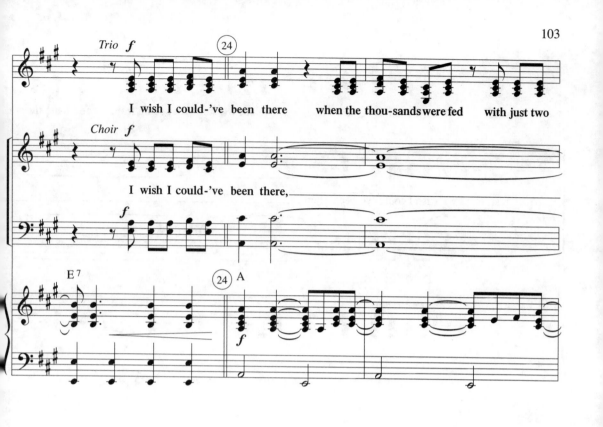

*Trio* ***f*** (24)

I wish I could-'ve been there when the thou-sands were fed with just two

*Choir* ***f***

I wish I could-'ve been there,

E7 (24) A

fish and some bread, and see the lit - tle boy pack - in' up the

lit - tle boy pack - in' up the

A

rest. I wish I could-'ve been there to see the lame that could leap, and hear the

rest. I wish I could-'ve been there.

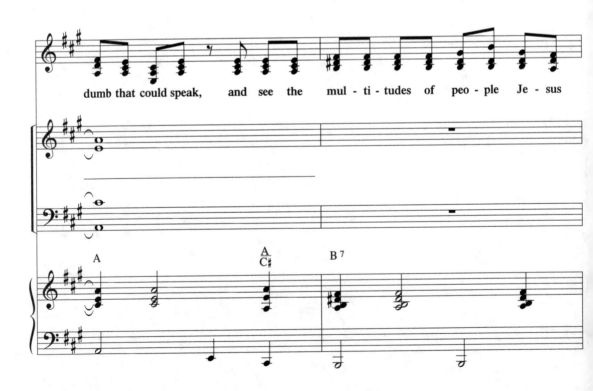

dumb that could speak, and see the mul - ti - tudes of peo - ple Je - sus

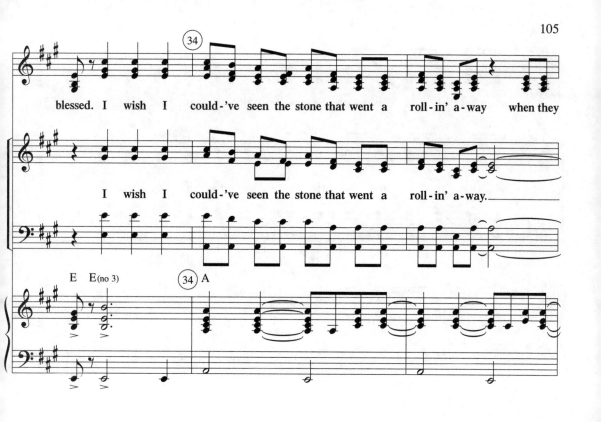

blessed. I wish I could-'ve seen the stone that went a roll-in' a-way when they

I wish I could-'ve seen the stone that went a roll-in' a-way.

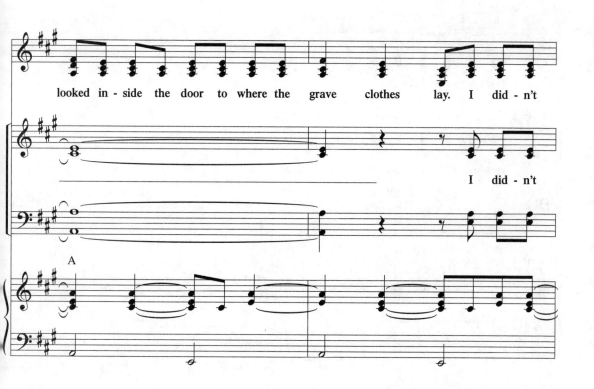

looked in-side the door to where the grave clothes lay. I did-n't

I did-n't

see, but I be-lieve that He as-cend-ed in the air, and I

real-ly wish I could-'ve been there! He com -

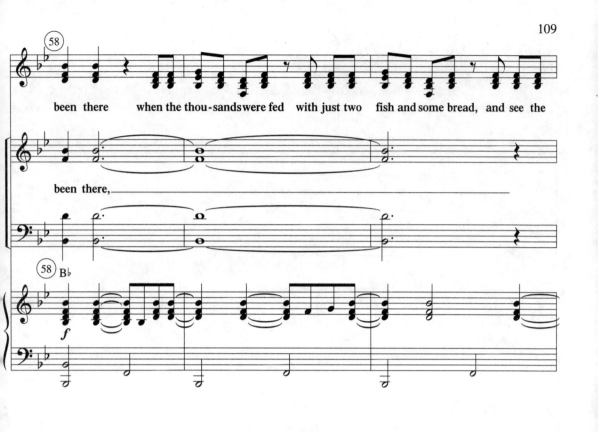

been there    when the thou-sands were fed    with just two    fish and some bread,    and see the

been there,_____

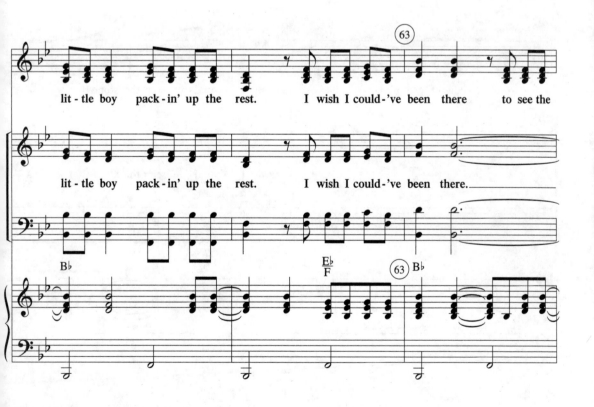

lit - tle boy    pack - in' up the    rest.    I wish I could-'ve been    there    to see the

lit - tle boy    pack - in' up the    rest.    I wish I could-'ve been    there._____

lame that could leap, and hear the dumb that could speak, and see the

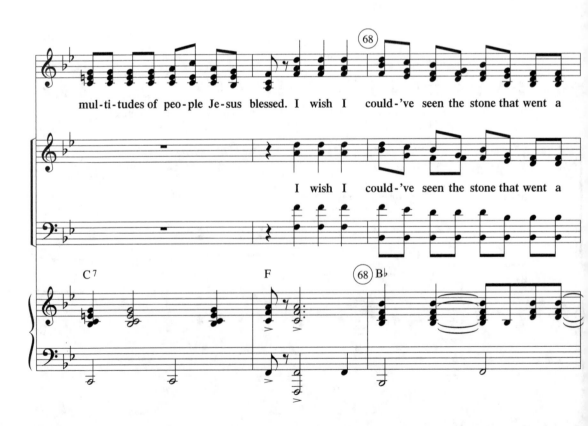

mul-ti-tudes of peo-ple Je-sus blessed. I wish I could-'ve seen the stone that went a

I wish I could-'ve seen the stone that went a

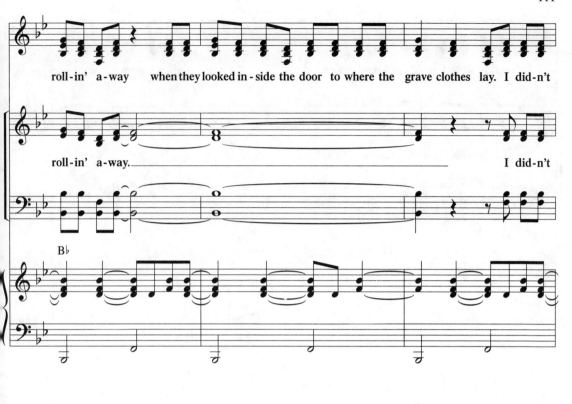

roll-in' a-way    when they looked in - side the door to where the grave clothes lay. I did-n't

roll-in'  a-way._____    I did-n't

see,   but   I   be - lieve  that  He   as - cend-ed   in   the   air,      and   I

see,   but   I   be - lieve  that  He   as - cend-ed   in   the   air,      and   I

real-ly wish I could-'ve been there! I wish I could-'ve

real-ly wish I could-'ve been there! I wish I could-'ve

C7    F    B♭    F♯7

been there when the thou-sands were fed with just two fish and some bread, and see the

been there,_____

B    B(no 3)

mf

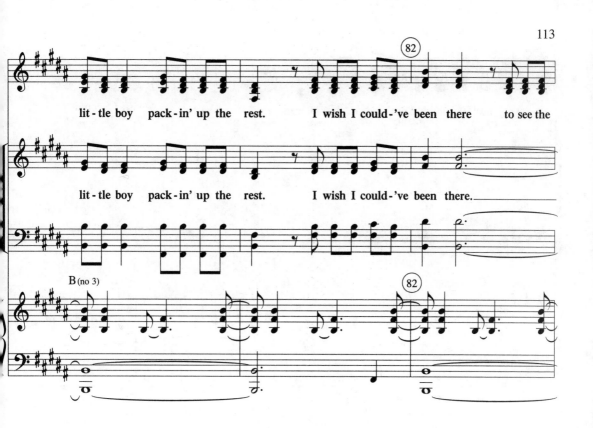

lit - tle boy pack - in' up the rest. I wish I could -'ve been there to see the

lit - tle boy pack - in' up the rest. I wish I could -'ve been there.

lame that could leap, and hear the dumb that could speak, and see the

mul-ti-tudes of peo-ple Je-sus blessed.    I    wish    I

I    wish    I

could-'ve seen the stone that went a    roll-in'  a-way    when they

could-'ve seen the stone that went a    roll-in'  a-way.

looked in - side the door to where the grave clothes lay. I did - n't

I did - n't

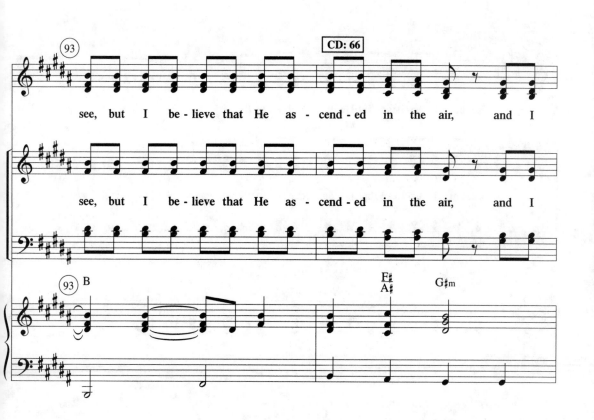

CD: 66

see, but I be - lieve that He as - cend - ed in the air, and I

see, but I be - lieve that He as - cend - ed in the air, and I

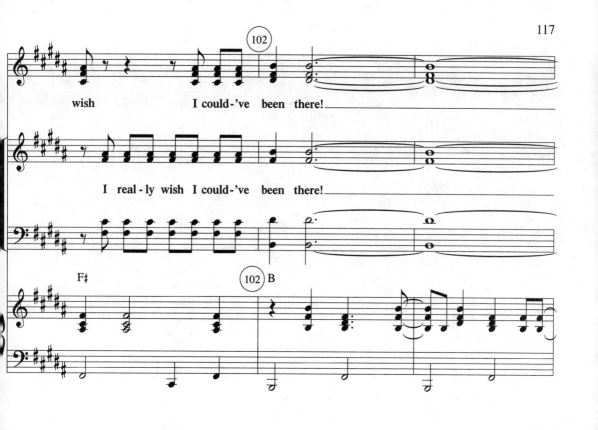

wish      I could-'ve   been   there!

I   real-ly   wish   I could-'ve   been   there!

I wish I could-'ve been there!

I wish I could-'ve been there!

118

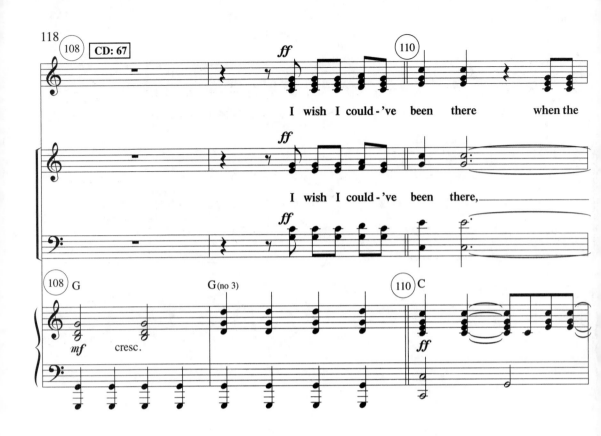

I wish I could-'ve been there when the

I wish I could-'ve been there,

thou-sands were fed with just two fish and some bread, and see the

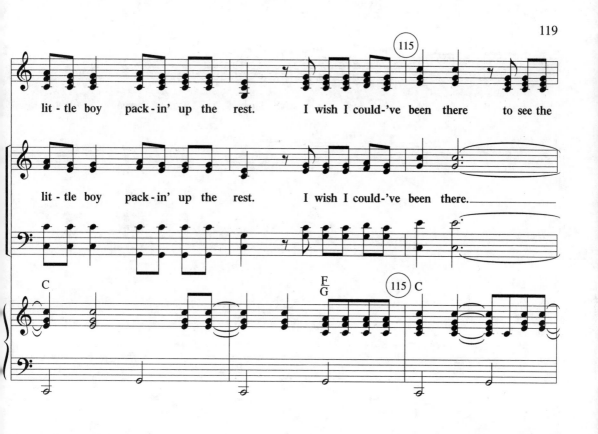

lit - tle boy    pack - in' up the    rest.         I wish I could-'ve been there        to see the

lit - tle boy    pack - in' up the    rest.         I wish I could-'ve been there.

lame that could leap,        and hear the    dumb that could speak,        and see the

mul - ti - tudes of peo - ple Je - sus blessed. I wish I

I wish I

could - 've seen the stone that went a roll - in' a - way when they

could - 've seen the stone that went a roll - in' a - way.

looked in - side the door to where the grave clothes lay. I did - n't

I did - n't

see, but I be - lieve that He as - cend - ed in the air, and I

see, but I be - lieve that He as - cend - ed in the air, and I

real - ly wish I could-'ve been there! I\_\_\_\_did - n't

real - ly wish I could-'ve been there!

D⁹  G  C

129 Trio

see, but I be - lieve that He as - cend - ed in the air, and I real - ly, real - ly

See, but I be - lieve that He as - cend - ed in the air, yes, I real - ly,

129 C

$\frac{G}{B}$  A m⁷  D⁷

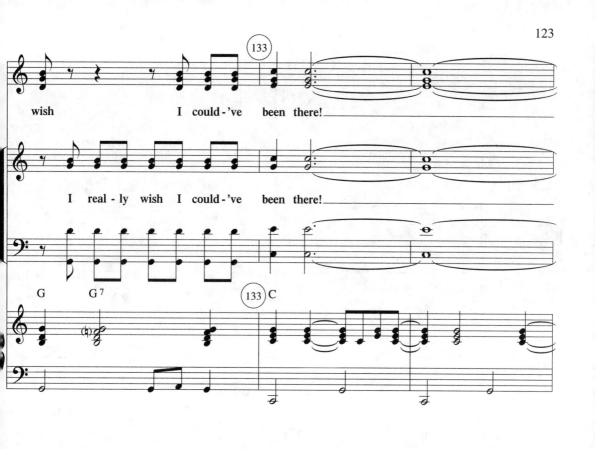

wish     I could-'ve    been there!

I   real-ly   wish   I could-'ve    been there!

I wish I could-'ve been there!

I wish I could-'ve been there!

# I Am God

*with*
## Fear Not My Child

Words and Music by
**TERY WILKINS**
*Arranged by Mike Speck,*
*Cliff Duren and Danny Zaloudik*

en - e - my___ sur - rounds___ you he can't harm_____ you. When you're

too tired to fight, don't give up hope. Don't let your heart

be - come trou - bled; Stand still and

Hear these words I say, I'm nev - er far a - way.

Stand still and know,

stand still and know! Fear not, My

*"Fear Not My Child"

Faster ♩ = ca. 66

child, I'm with you al - ways. I know how to care. Child, I'm al - ways there. I

130

Slower ♩ = ca. 60

love you.   You  be-long_____ to me._____

B♭(no 3)   N.C.   Fm7   B♭7   E♭   B♭2/D

ff  Slower

Hear these words  I   say,   I'm  nev - er far   a-way.

Cm7   F7   D7   Gm2   Gm   Gm7

Stand   still   and  know,_____   stand  still   and

Cm7   B♭/D   F7sus   F7   Cm7   B♭/D

*Unison*

know_____ I am God,_____

*Unison*

*Divisi*

_____ I am God,_____

*Divisi*

*rit.*

I am God!_____

*rit.*

# Spirit of the Living God

*with*
Fresh Anointing

Words and Music by
**DANIEL IVERSON**
*Arranged by Mike Speck,*
*Cliff Duren and Danny Zaloudik*

134

CD: 77

Je - sus, His will, His way. Lord, we need a fresh a-

noint - ing. We can-not bor - row from yes - ter - day. Come and

feed us, Ho - ly Spir - it, teach us of Je - sus, His will, His

CD: 78

Choir tacet to end

fall      fresh   on      me.

# At His Feet

*with*
Press on
I Pledge Allegiance to the Lamb

Words and Music by
LARRY PETREE
*Arranged by Mike Speck,*
*Cliff Duren and Danny Zaloudik*

times we get___so wea - ry of the bur-dens that__we bear.___

**PLEASE NOTE: Copying of this product is NOT covered by CCLI licenses. For CCLI information call 1-800-234-2446.**

*"Press on"
(28) Slightly faster ♩ = ca. 72

In Je - sus' name we press on.

In Je - sus'

name we press on. Dear

*"I Pledge Allegiance to the Lamb"

A little slower ♩ = ca. 64

146

# I'm a Soldier

*Final Reprise*

Words and Music
Unknown
*Arranged by Mike Speck,
Cliff Duren and Danny Zaloudik*

(to pg. 148, meas. 5)

ar-my of the Lord, I'm a sol - dier in the ar - my.___ I'm a

ar - my of the Lord. I'm a sol - dier in the

ar - my of the Lord.

# Fresh Anointing
### *(For Congregational Use)*

Words and Music by
SYDNEY G. COBLE

Lord, we need a fresh a-noint-ing; We can-not bor-row from yes-ter-day. Come and feed us, Ho-ly Spir-it, Teach us of Je-sus, His will, His way.

FOR INFORMATION AND BOOKINGS CONTACT:

Mike Speck Ministries

P. O. Box 2609

Lebanon, TN 37088

(615) 449-1888